ALSO BY SIMMONS B. BUNTIN

Riverfall (Salmon Poetry, 2005)

Bloom
Simmons B. Buntin

salmonpoetry

Published in 2010 by
Salmon Poetry
Cliffs of Moher, County Clare, Ireland
Website: www.salmonpoetry.com
Email: info@salmonpoetry.com

Copyright © Simmons B. Buntin, 2010

ISBN 978-1-907056-49-9

All rights reserved. No part of this publication may be reproduced or transmitted in any form or by any means, electronic or mechanical, including photography, recording, or any information storage or retrieval system, without permission in writing from the publisher. The book is sold subject to the condition that it shall not, by way of trade or otherwise, be lent, resold or otherwise circulated without the publisher's prior consent in any form of binding or cover other than that in which it is published and without a similar condition, including this condition, being imposed on the subsequent purchaser.

Cover photography: *Simmons B. Buntin*
Cover design: *Siobhán Hutson*
Typesetting: *Siobhán Hutson*
Printed in England by imprint*digital*.net

for my daughters
Ann-Elise and Juliet

and for their mother
Billie

and in memory of my mother
Diana Anne-Marie Estelle Gunilla von Schinkel Bancroft

Acknowledgements

I am grateful to the editors of the following journals in which some of these poems first appeared, sometimes in a different format:

The Aurorean: "Promenade"
Because I Told You So: Poems on the Happiness and Crappiness of Parenthood: "Shower"
Corridors: "Amazon.com," "Antler among Poppies," "Sting," "Thorn"
Isotope: A Journal of Literary Nature and Science Writing: "Angelfish," "In May I Consider My Websites"
Freshwater: "Arc"
Hawk & Whippoorwill: "Bosque," "Safehouse"
Kyoto Journal: "Plastic"
The LBJ: Avian Life, Literary Arts: "Flight"
The Manhattan Review: "Her Mission of Light," "The Vernacular of Fire and Rain"
North American Review: "Friday Afternoon"
Orion: "Wild Mint"
Palehouse: "Radiance"
Re)verb: "Whether You are Listening or You are Reading"
Potomac Review: "Box"
Salamander: "A Garden of Bones"
shaking like a mountain: "Desert Jazz"
Snowy Egret: "The Gift"
South Dakota Review: "Shine"
Southwestern American Literature: "Cardinals, Sabino Canyon"
Spiral Orb: "On Considering the Universe, Sweet Acacias Blooming between Sidewalk and Street"
Stimulus Respond: "Ritual"
Sugar House Review: "Question"
Terrain.org: A Journal of the Built & Natural Environments: "Float," "Opuntia"
TIFERET: A Journal of Spiritual Literature (2010 Poetry Contest Finalist): "Home and Back Again"
Versal: "Dining in SoHo"
Whiskey Island Magazine: "Flare"

My deepest thanks and love go out to my wife Billie and daughters Ann-Elise and Juliet, blossoms all, who continue to provide inspiration to me—as a husband and father, poet, and member of life's rich and curious community.

Special thanks go out to Alison Hawthorne Deming, whose input on and conversations about many of these poems have been both lively and essential—for me and the poems. And special thanks to Scott Calhoun for his thoughtful review of this book, and his friendship along the way, to Emily Wall for her considerate review and comments, and to Jamison Crabtree, Jennifer McStotts, and Mare Smith for their final reviews.

Much gratitude is also owed to the following people and organizations, who continue to help guide poetry and art for me and many others in the Sonoran desert and beyond: H. Emerson Blake, Hannah Fries, and the Orion Society; Gail Browne, Cybele Knowles, and the many good folks at the University of Arizona Poetry Center; Melissa Buckheit, Kristen Nelson, and the Edge Reading Series at Casa Libre en la Solana; Wendy Burk; Douglas Carlson; Miriam Marty Clark; Christopher Cokinos; Philip Fried; Deborah Fries; Suzanne Frischkorn; Frank Gohlke; Andrew C. Gottlieb; William Keener; Bruce Kirschner; Eric Magrane; Kathryn Miles; William Pitt Root; David Rothenberg; Elizabeth Salper; Derek Sheffield; R.T. Smith; Pamela Uschuk; and Jake Adam York.

Travels inspiring some of these poems were partly funded by the Arizona Commission on the Arts and the Tucson Pima Arts Council. Many thanks.

Finally, my continued thanks to Jessie Lendennie, Siobhán Hutson, and Jean Kavanagh at Salmon Poetry, a genuine beacon for poetry in Europe, North America, and across the globe. Your support, friendship, and superb craftsmanship (craftswomanship!) are irreplaceable.

Contents

Whether You are Listening or You are Reading	13

1. Shine

Shine	17
Bosque	18
Plastic	19
Drawing	21
Friday Afternoon	23
In May I Consider My Websites	24
Amazon.com	25
Shower	26
Desert Jazz	28
The Gift	29
Ritual	31
A Garden of Bones	33
Flight	34
Cardinals, Sabino Canyon	36
Story	38
Arc	40

2. Flare

Flare	43
Wild Mint	44
Angelfish	45
The Vernacular of Fire and Rain	46
Home and Back Again	47
Animal Logic	49
On Considering the Universe, Sweet Acacias Blooming between Sidewalk and Street	50
Promenade	51

Float	52
Safehouse	53
Question	54
Box	56
Dining in SoHo	57
Radiance	58
Antler among Poppies	59
Sting	60
Thorn	62
Opuntia	65
Her Mission of Light	66

3. Inflorescence

Inflorescence	71
NOTES	85
GLOSSARY	89
ABOUT THE AUTHOR	95
DIGITAL RESOURCES	97

Whether You are Listening or You are Reading

there is a poem for you and it may
be like this poem for my wife

who listens to a podcast and sometimes
laughs so hard her earbuds drop

and she looks at me and smiles, shares
the story of the actress and her monologue

or the man who unwittingly confesses
his most embarrassing moment on the radio

before she tucks the tiny white speakers
back into her ears. On the other side

of the table I slip into a book of poems,
sometimes nodding or clicking my tongue

in agreement before looking away
to the shelves across the room, the white

antler discovered in a saffron field,
or the photographs of my daughters

who are asleep now in their rooms,
Juliet curled beneath a quilt of flowers,

Ann-Elise bent across her black blanket,
foot draped over the bedframe, the house quiet

except for those burbling springs of laughter
and the murmur of turning pages

as I think of you again, listening or reading—
the poem paused by the person you love.

1. Shine

Shine

Pouring the black light into every crevice,
we follow the thick vertebrae of the wall

until the moon and bats rise—
until the purple radiance fills the night. There

and *there*, all at once, the poisonous scorpions shine,
their exoskeletons like intricate green

imps stealing moths at twilight.
We keep their gruesome glow in our minds

and on our tongues as we talk
through the empty hours of the drive home:

the dark mountain pass, the pressing lights
of the city, the dim lane leading

to our house—and then brake hard
at the tangled braid of red and yellow and

black. Eyes open and shining, jaw heavy
with venom, the coral snake's body

is bent upon itself, rolled tight from the quick black
wheels of the day. Gathering ourselves

now into the car, into the silent rooms
of our house, there is a violet

light pouring over everything and nothing,
like that last terrible night in Eden

when every sharp animal rushed to hide
in all the exposed crevices of the world.

Bosque

Bosque del Apache National Wildlife Refuge, New Mexico
January 1, 2009

Not the riotous snow geese or the cyclone
    of tungsten wings beneath the dawn's red rise.

Not the silent teals drawn like musical notes
    across the vellum of the marsh.

Not even the scarlet-capped cranes slowly rowing
    above copper hills. Rather, my daughters,

bundled in bright plumage on the observation deck
    —the unfathomable water glazed in blue ice, the ruby

woods distant and luring—their own capped heads
    and arms lifted skyward, and rising.

Plastic

After Midway: Message from the Gyre,
photographs by Chris Jordan, September 2009

Children are plastic
the doctor says
as he cuts away
the splint of my daughter's
shin, revealing a scar
curved like the forewing
of an albatross
as it levels over open
ocean—carved
by the shattering
door, the plate glass
scattering like sunlight
on waves as she
dove through that hard
reality, her soft body
easily severed:
                plastic
like the sensuous
bottle of soda
she slides
into her backpack
after school, the air sighing
from the red lid
before the final twist,
bottle surfacing
in the recycling bin,
cap sinking
in the day's trash:
                plastic
as in malleable, fix-
able, her pale flesh

healing in the dark
corridor of the cast, dead
skin black as the ocean
at night, sloughing away
like the feathers
of lying birds:
     plastic
like the odd collage
of litter discovered body
after decomposing body
in the Midway Atoll,
dull plumage and bleached
vertebrae vivid
against the contraband
of buttons and bottle caps,
combs and cartridges,
bobbles and lighters lifted
from the flotsam
of the Pacific—
bright bobbers resembling
the fish and quick squid
the albatross catch
for insatiable chicks:
     plastic
curved by the luminous
sweep of the sea,
curved through genetic
structure, curved
into crisp gills
and blue beaks
and the mouths
of children severed
like so many seabirds
by the dazzling waves.

Drawing

*On the 40th Anniversary of the Dropping of the Bomb
Hiroshima, August 6, 1985*

What could I say at sixteen,
the plaza thick with tourists
like me, when a local teacher asked
for my response to the bomb—
I mean, he said, was it right?

What could I say except
the loss of lives was terrible,
of course, but didn't
the bomb in the end save
more than it took? No emotion
from the instructor whose English
seemed sharper than my own,
whose students assembled
in a smart line of white blouses
and blue skirts: tall ships
swaying on the horizon.

And what could I say earlier
in the day when, beneath the sharp
outline of empty dome, I saw
the smudge of atomic shadows—
the two anti-shadows
of sitting lovers who, when
the bomb blossomed
overhead, could not comprehend
the unbearable light
before its radiance raged
into darkness? How many
died before reaching sixteen,
before flying around the world
to wander the wide plazas
of those remembering
or trying to forget?

But that is the old argument
I cannot overcome, the guilt
I did not bear as the elephant
eye of the teacher's camera
caught my awkward
pause, the held moment
when the air between us bent
under the inconceivable weight
of a city's despair.

I vanished then
into my own memory, how
at the gates of Kyoto
and Osaka castle and below
the gleaming glass of Tokyo
I sketched an idea
of Japanese history
all samurais and dragons,
curved swords and flaming
tongues, a crowd of people
gathering at every trainstop
and bustling café to glimpse
this straw-haired boy's
illustrations, asking what
I was drawing
before turning away.

What could I say
that they had not already
heard or since seen
in the ink laid to paper,
my hand scraping the intricate
black lines of stitched
armor and shield—
lines crossing the vellum
like the highways
of a city map, sudden smudges
at the center before the sky
blooms forever into fiery night?

Friday Afternoon

for Ann-Elise

Perhaps it was the rare day of rain or uneven
weave of my walk as I arrived home after
hours on the courts, blue shorts

swimming around my knees, that caused
you to condemn my skinny legs: I mean *really*
skinny, dad, you said, kicking me

back to my freshman year and the bully
who called me *flamingo*, the name sticking
that entire Florida year, though my legs

were neither scaled nor scarlet—
which caused me to study the sleek white
heron stalking the high school ponds and how

I wanted then (as perhaps now) to draw my legs
tighter, to share the black reeds and dagger-
quick beak of that pearly bird, to launch

into the sultry air, water trailing like a whip
behind me. And wouldn't you, my slim
daughter, also like to split the earthly skin

of your body so that your own thin and hollow
bones could catch this wind and lift you up
and over the day's swirling storm? Or consider

the breakaway crane, feathers thick
and gray like the clouds now spilling
over the mountains, flower-stem legs

flowing behind the vase of his body
in flight, the neck not crooked but firm
and straight, head aimed forward: true north.

In May I Consider My Websites

My client reminds me that the April coupon
is still online, though it's mid-May, and though
there is a white-winged dove at the feeder,
just arrived from Mexico or maybe Belize.

And that reminds me of the Mexican birds-of-paradise
fanning the backyard in yellow and red, the orange
globemallow now past prime at their rooted and clenching
toes. Beyond the wall, the scarlet ocotillo flowers

are fading to brown, lost in the arid silhouette
of the mountains seemingly painted behind them.
Which reminds me of the trail my daughters and I
hiked late last month, past aromatic creosote—

the rains lingering this winter—past slate and prickly
pear that shine like windows in the sunlight. The view
from here is, of course, gorgeous; and that
reminds me of the website I'm crafting for my neighbor's

bed and breakfast, with its elegant landscaping
and utterly modern IKEA décor. They are sure to be
a hit—the square tables and chairs and atmosphere,
I mean—which reminds me of the coupon, again,

and now that it's half past the month of May (or more)
I better get to it, as I pause at the front room's
inviting window, reminding me—as a Gila flicker
drops in—of the yard's single saguaro, open and blooming.

Amazon.com

Spooky my wife says. *They know my secrets.*
It's true I think. This morning, as the light scratches
across the keyboard, I browse the homepage and find
my own glittering recommendations: cherry-handled
rose pruners, their glossy alloy beaks spring-tuned;
new music by the Silos, a Top 10 on Dan Steely's
alt-college country rock list; and the books,
the wonderful unfathomable books—three or three-thousand
sensuously bound classics of love, mystery,
and safe passage into Sonora, Mexico.
I hover above No. 1,897,615: *Click here*
to purchase.

        Why not? Even the Pinacate Press
in Lukeville, Arizona knows its wares are sung to me,
the guy idling eagerly outside Sonoyta's port-of-entry,
travel guide buried in the trunk, the air burning
with recommendations.

Shower

Our house is full of ladybugs. My daughter has released the whole lot, the profit of an afternoon's unwavering work: busy opals in red and black, black and gray, caught beneath palo verde shade and poppy sheath. In the insect box she lays silver leaves of guava, gentle shoots of yellow sage. As she gathers them one by one, cradled in the warm chalice of her hand, I read Irish poetry and observe the garden: the bluebells are fading, their indigo petals turn to glass and stain the desert floor. The agave sends a single martyred spike to the sky.

Back on earth, she gathers more and more. The bug house is filling, buzzing like a midsummer hive.

In my book: spring snow in Dublin and scarves of silver and green. In our garden: she is

absolutely floating—*forty!* Glowing
like a Chinese lantern, like the

sudden hillside of Indian paint-
brush, she races inside, opens

the box, and showers
the room with

pure red
joy.

Desert Jazz

*Take four steps left and four
steps right*, my daughter sings
as she draws her new
dance on the wall's white
board—bluegrass to blame
for it all: the house concert
last night, the buzzing
of the twelve-string
as she nuzzled into the camp
chair beneath the star-plucked
desert sky. Playing
the album this evening—
its fluid harmonica and slide
guitar—she sings *do-si-do*
followed by *slide left* and
slide right, two steps each
as she glides to the final
do-si-do of the dance
called Jazz Square. After
the banjo gives way
to clarinet and after
my daughter gives way
to acoustic folk and then
to the sweet and solemn blues
she knows at once
she's always known,
a cool brass horn rolls
out the gelled moon—
bees humming in their dark hives,
owls swinging their bass
pendulums from the rooftops,
coyotes singing wild jazz
from the box canyons
of the intoxicating night.

The Gift

On the night of my fortieth birthday
the ringtail swept over ductwork

and steel, watched as we served
cake and chardonnay.

Of all the coveted gifts,
how could I wish for more

than those obsidian eyes, sharp face
and paws, the sudden leap to dark

rafters making the entire room gasp?
What silent passage had he found

into our corner café, what conduit
of wild commerce channeled

his return? The evening after
our discovery I crept over to catch

the flash of striped tail before the brokers
closed the deal and sealed the pipes

and high sconces for good.
Was he out hunting cats

in the courtyard, or venomous
serpents among thistle and sage?

Or perhaps he foresaw the new tenants
and fled, weaving through walkways

of granite and slate, through walled
suburban gardens, through even

the lonely café of my mind,
climbing the blue ductwork

of the bountiful night, a feral
ceiling of stars at the edge of my reach.

Ritual

In the amber shadows of the evening
there is a ritual that fills the rooms

and soft mouths of our children:
What will you dream tonight?

I am the blue moth, our older daughter
says, in a garden of glass roses.

I flit between petals and stems
and call it poetry, she grins. Her sister too

is old enough to share: we climb the backs
of unicorns and fly to the forest, to the edges

of dark trees, where I pour the waiting tea.
Each night she speaks the same dream

but her sister is no longer a moth, is
instead a snowy eagle: landing in a snag,

she watches the magical mares.
It is possible they are the best of friends

or the eagle is a tyrant—a snake
in its sinister beak—the big sister who tricks

her sibling from dollars and dolls.
There is—in these dreams, in the deep

corners of our home—always movement
and the lifting up, the transcendence.

We know of course that one night our ritual
will diminish. One night my wife and I will settle

into our own dreams, where at the edge
of the woods a silver raptor sews the sky

as a fine charger spins the land, rolling
and rolling into luminous sleep.

A Garden of Bones

If there are weeds in the yard's corner garden
    they are fine as feathers, white

as desert quartz, strung from the buried coil
    of snake my daughters discovered

dead at the edge of our street.
    If there are weeds in the blue garden

of the dawn, drawn like vertebrae
    beneath thorny mesquite, they are plump

as peppers, thick as the red rush of arroyo
    in flood—bound to the delicate box

of desert tortoise found crushed
    against the alley wall.

If there are weeds in the simple garden we chiseled
    from caliche, they reach with needle-

thin fingers beyond the river and its bent
    bridge, flit like the bat wing-caught

and wind-stripped at the gate's black
    latch. With each burial we mark

the dark plot with stones, a small ceremony,
    and think of the industrious creatures

and the decaying museum of their bones.
    How now can we turn the body

of the soil to plant spring bulbs?
    What if the weeds tap sweet marrow and bloom?

Flight

1.

Two birds sketched
by my daughter: red
as finches in the feeder,
plump as doves in a storm.
The male is caught
beak open; his mate hovers
on locked wings
above the lip
of their nest. No chick
or egg, no sun or dazzle
like the yard's swift
chat. No movement at all
except fluid limbs
among a carnival
of leaves.

2.

This evening my wife
drives to the emergency

room and the long uneasy
wait. The nervous

bird of her heart is leaving, is
pressing into and beyond the night.

Tail lights flash like summer
tanagers.

My daughter believes the gray
owl of our neighbor's yard

can call her mother
home, weave the hollow-

boned heart back into the nest
of her pale breast.

3.

Late last summer
we startled a pair
of sparrows
above the porch door.
One flew
in wild circles

beneath the bright bulb.
The other
pitched straight
into a pillar: into sweet
jasmine: into the desolate
suburban night.

Cardinals, Sabino Canyon

I was scared, she says, and walks a shadow's length
to my side—between the high road and guardrail,

the ledge and sharp rocks below. At seven,
scared is relative: the low weed's thorn under thumb,

a bumblebee drunk on the pattern of her dress.
Sugarbug, I say, think of it as *adventure*.

But I should explain: in the gauzy morning light
we drive up the high canyon to hike down an empty trail.

The signs—if you believe such things—are all bright:
the paint-red cardinal on ocotillo, a turquoise

lizard among desert marigold. It isn't until
the trail dissolves that fear begins.

> *In 1987, above rapids*
> > *downstream a man*
> > > *with a daughter*
> > > > *of his own rescues*
> > > > > *a stranded girl*
> > > > > > *before falling.*

We climb, hands and feet among thistled acacia, Sabino
Creek well below. The thick snake of the road courses

above us: we can hear the trams but cannot find the trail.
I want to go back, she cries. We are just about there, I lie.

> *In 2001, a mountain lion*
> > *leaps from the brush*
> > > *and though her father*
> > > > *hurls himself*
> > > > > *at the curving muscle*
> > > > > > *his daughter is gone.*

Pressed against the scarp, I lift her above loose rock
but slip and slice my knee. The blood is like a cardinal

dropping feathers as it lifts. I want to go back, she demands—
but then we make it to the broken steps that lead I swear

to the road above. I can see it, she says, and breathes
once more as I raise her over the rail, over the scarlet

penstemon that bleeds across the pavement—a cardinal
calling from the canyon's very source.

Story

for Juliet

The story I thought
I could tell
begins in the sweet water

of your mother's womb
before rushing to knife-
bright air,

lungs expunged
and arm bent hard
across your chest,

its imprint painted
as birth mark
during labor; your sister

three years old
and terrified:
wiping mother's face

with the cool
linen, convincing colorless
lips to take ice

chips between my counts,
before that terribly
beautiful final push—

plum blue
umbilical cord intact,
placenta washing

finally out before
nurturing the yard's
palo verde, before

your desert
blue eyes open,
unfocused

but clear, like
the weather today
as you bicycle

in the long
afternoon shade
of the trees,

asking about the day
you were born
nine years ago

and floating
on sleek pedals like
a wind-born flower

through the perfumed
lines of the story
now yours to keep or tell.

Arc

If there is an art
to scaling desert
boulders in bare feet
it is this: my daughter,
eleven, tosses her sandals
to prickly pear
and mesquite, pries
knee into crevice,
and presses onto the sun-
drunk surface
like a lizard revealed,
hair blazing
in late afternoon
light, pants hitched
mid-calf, a hard
look of fear
and determination
before fingers and feet
release to the flat
wind, time slowed
by her sudden
leap to sharp granite
and the improbable
landing, only a thin
necklace of blood
on her ankle, red
like the thorn-guarded
flower, the arc
of a girl's first desire.

2. Flare

Flare

South of Arizona 86, we slow at a sudden
field of gold-poppies and dappled bladderpod.

Already their heads are closing—already the dark
cape of desert sky calls them home.

How like that roadside gouache we are, I say:
born of the mad summer storms, rain-soaked

and rooted like ravens on the scarp's red slope.
And like the single white lily drinking

the last brushstroke of sunlight, you say, flaring
now to rise again next spring.

Wild Mint

Did you know that in my hand-sized guide you are shelved
among the *Blue odd-shaped flowers?* You, the purple coyote
in the field—your feet licking the moist soil, releasing

the slow and the sweet. And did you know in the volcanic slide
of the red and solemn hills there is a gully grinning between broken
teeth and in the palate of light where you and I live, foraging

among the brittlebush and saxifrage, I have peeled the dark earth
for a mad glimpse of your pure white flesh? Have you not also
felt the blue mustangs wrapping the rivers of their hooves

through our canyons, the cottonwoods closing in around us—
indeed, the entire mountain dropping its shoulders to green shadow?
There is nothing to reference the long roll of the melancholy night,

nothing except perhaps for the passage on page five-hundred
ninety-seven: *The dark teas made from the leaves of this intricately
fragrant herb treat ailments and pause the pain of childbirth.*

Even now we hear the coyote's howls, low from beneath the hidden
ledge, followed by the sudden yips of blind and naked pups.

Angelfish

How she navigates
the deep corners
of her world—
the evening's sea-blue
glass reflecting
green hills & dark
clouds—

how the manna
falls, flaked
& curling, to the open
mouths of catfish,
the conspiracy of scarlet
cichlids—

how finally
the fluorescent light strikes
her flashing fins:
the sudden fusing
of silver wings & the flat
sky peeling as she rises:
clouds shining

like gated cities in the holy
coins of her eyes.

The Vernacular of Fire and Rain

These words cannot hold a candle
to the sprawling flames on the mountainside—
the venomous flare

asping through bent and blackened trees.
They cannot kill two birds with a single
stone, even stone as sudden fireball:

the wrath of a thousand granite giants
from the mountain's stirring core. And I'm afraid
they don't hold water, like those great

gray whales weaving the sky's torrential sea—
the tipping planes that dive and spray.
Listen: I have seen the shotgun scatter

of glowing birds as the ground, sloping
to nothing, explodes and all becomes a dark-
less night, a mad glory of wings pounding

the burning limbs, abandoned cabins, the lit
and frozen eyes of the forest come alive.
All I can offer, in the end—an end without

syllables, without even the solidity
of consonants—is that it's not the heat, it's
the humidity. So when the rain chants down

like a new vocabulary, when the tongue celebrates
the wet vowels of the dawn, when
finally the fiery blanket draws back—

the rock and the branch, the mountain
and the sky sing fully this radiant cleansing:
this virgin chorus that marks the immaculate day.

Home and Back Again

for Alison Hawthorne Deming

On the day I learned of your partner's
ocular stroke I thought myself back

to the fall potluck where his arrival
delighted us all: a radiance I'd seen

only once before, at the Yaqui deer dance
off South Thirty-Ninth, where he leaned

back against Easter chants as the water
drums scooped mouthfuls of air

and my own breath; he leaned back
against you and even the student looking

and not looking could see the other
dance, the door to your own flower world

where the savage hunt and sweet reward
hang between the thick windows

of the desert at night. Thought myself
back to our first meeting, those silver

blue eyes, the white beard shining
in the afternoon's slow exhale,

how we talked trail and arroyo, the houses
built on the last perfect urban edge: ours.

Thought back to the day as a boy
I sliced my thigh on barbed wire

as I fled a shirtless man with wild
hair I swore couldn't be chasing me

through that high-walled wash but was,
was walking at the same rate I was running,

was running in my mind but my memory
staggers there. I escaped, sure,

but what I want to say is
the chase keeps me watching even now,

how in the shimmering silver stretches
of the arroyo I see some wild face

in the creosote or bare-root mesquite.
What I want to say is after

the final Yaqui song and after you drove
away, the old dancer slipped

off the antlers and drenched leggings,
the deer skin and thumb-smooth rattles,

but kept the blindfold tight. He turned
then and sang the sun above

the freeway, blinding us all for the wild
plunge home, and back again.

Animal Logic

> *Here, we, where the white wood stands,*
> *together we meet,*
> *together we will talk about this animal.*
>
> — from an untitled Yaqui deer song
> by Don Jesús Yoilo'i

This animal that is a god, or God.

❧

This god that is ever-present, or ever-distant.

❧

This god that is in all things created—
the wilderness, the moon and sun,
the pulsing galaxies beyond—
or the god that is the Genesis
and the Exodus, no longer a god.

❧

This god that is a universe, at once
in and of everything,
or the god that is a machine,
our machine, an enterprise
of self-replicating technology,
the temple and its congregation
of inventors.

❧

This god in the indigo eyes
of my daughters, or the god
of plague and terror and genocide.

❧

This god of indifference.

On Considering the Universe, Sweet Acacias Blooming between Sidewalk and Street

    Trunks glow blue
among yellow flowers:
    whole constellations of them
in the dark branches
        of the night.

Promenade

Night again
                     & imagine my surprise

      when the lantern caught
                                  the stems at eye level
& tiny moths burst
               from the blooms:

            as if they had waited all evening:

    as if light was the final pull
                             & release

Float

At the wilder edge of our street,
    across the street, a car:
        abandoned, windows down

or gone completely. Every day I watch
    its devolution: how the silent
        tendrils of lantana seduce the open

rims and exhausted vents,
    how a taillight-pink penstemon
        tumbles through the checkered trellis

of the trunk and a curved-billed
    thrasher steals the dashboard
        wires for its crazy backseat nest.

Finally, neighbor Tom has had enough
    and calls the salvage yard, where
        a pulsing crowd of well-wishers—

red-headed flickers, blue buntings,
    white evening primrose—yawps wildly
        as the parade's latest entry glides on by.

Safehouse

Against the moon, bruised
      in ruddy eclipse,
            I find the thorntree's nest

abandoned, a tangle
      of bluestem & sage.
            Last spring the mourning

doves fled the battered roost,
      the brood lost
            early, shells weathered

to white dust. New seekers
      now, as sparrows tease
            the bent leaves & mottled

wrens weave moonlight
      to madness in their quick
            & raucous wit.

The laughter calls
      the great-horned owl,
            cast like a gargoyle

on the horizon of rooftop—
      eyes red as the shadowed
            moon, as the earth's own

waning. A low cry
      & the songbirds drop
            to cold silence,

the nest cracked open
      to the ravenous night—
            the safehouse sold.

Question

I know you can answer
        this question, she said:
                If a person lives near an arroyo

will scorpions scuttle up
        and into the house? Turning
                the question on its chitinous back,

I said: If a scorpion lives
        in an arroyo, will humans hurry
                out and into the wash? Consider

the brilliant honeycombs
        discovered last week
                in our patio wall—

six wax lattices loaded
        with honey, the hive humming
                through early spring days,

bees slipping in threes
        and fours from the stucco crack
                before we sealed the sweet

cavity with lavender and caulk.
        Even past midnight
                the lit door behind me lures

dark creatures: geckos dart
        along the doormat, a heavy beetle
                hurls itself at the shuddering glass.

The scorpions have their own
        concerns, scaling low branches
                to snare the skittish moths

or pressing into crevices
        beyond roadrunner's reach.
                And my curious friend

who thinks I can answer
        her question?
                She draws back

from each stone and stem
        knowing every hand burns
                for the perilous sting.

Box

> *A house is a box of secrets.*
> — Frank Gohlke

Not the golden key to the city
or the diary inlaid with mother-of-pearl
but the tarnished pass to the pool
gone missing. We've scoured

the kitchen drawers with their rattling
knives, searched every cold
pocket on the crowded coat rack.
We could scale the high gate

but what of our neighbors, what
would they think? Back to the box
of secrets, then, to tally the damnable
list: remote control, of course,

and the finely drawn invitation
to a cousin's wedding dissolved
long ago. If only we could unlock
the bright closet of every dark token.

If only we could spring the pool's board,
split the glass skin for the treasure
at its depths. Or returning home
we'd heave the concrete floor—the old

slab cleaving as the soil's rich scent
curls through the house, coiling
over us like the coffin's silk lining,
burying ourselves in secrets unrevealed.

Dining in SoHo

after William Carlos Williams

Instead of the restaurant
    on Mulberry & Spring
the gutter

Instead of the staircase
    the brick cracked
& revealing

This evening as rain
    pocked the streets
in pools ringing

& wrung with humming
    lights
—yellow & red—

a hunched
    starling lit
on the glossy wire

Buoyed & wind-
   blown its sharp eye
split our table

into halves
1) A storm bent
    on breaking

2) Runoff caught
    in a crosswalk ir-
    idescent in its rising

Radiance

If the day ended in the sweet
        and tangled tenor
                of tanager and wren

or in mountains burning—
        a sunset of scarlet
                and bronze—

or in a searing star, a white-
        hot needle across an indigo sky,
                then perhaps I could forget

the close friends announcing
        their move to Peru,
                forget the pierced goshawk

at the base of the wall,
        forget even the diagnosis
                of a neighbor's blossoming

disease. How could any of us divine
        the unfathomable day, sing
                swift radiance from impossible night?

Antler among Poppies

On a field of desert poppies
    I learned to watch
        for the finer forms:

cholla spines spilling
    from a body all joints,
        or barrel cactus shin-deep, wild

hyacinth twined
    among wicked thorns.
        Who but the buzzards

truly survey the land?
    Who but the scythe-winged
        spirits know the old, old blade

that is death?
    This afternoon that curved
        shadow caught my heel,

or so I thought. I bent to find
    an antler, three-pronged and bleached
        among the sulfur blooms.

What I want to say
    is that I left the sharp prize
        after measuring its heft.

What I think is that one
    sacrifice across a plain
        of seasonal brilliance is enough.

Sting

                Pocked
then sealed
        the under-
                ground wombs
of Sonoran bees
        with names like
                Diadosia ronconis &
Melissodes paucipuncta
        are at a loss
                for profit
That is there is
        no honey &
                no hive—
a thousand species
        solitary
                except that ritual
that flower-mad dance
        that risk of sting
                on sweet sting
& in a desert
        in Israel
                ground-dwelling bees
milk
        the nectar from
                rich blooms
A thousand
        species there
                too
& like our
        Tumacacori valley
                also a wall
to keep a people
        out—
                & also too high
for the low-flying bees

                        to cross
                                        or cross-fertilize
            the crops
                        grown south
                                        to raise
            northern profits
                        and feed
                                        northern mouths
            & how's that
                        for fertile
                                        justice

Thorn

> *But he that dares not grasp the thorn*
> *Should never crave the rose.*
>   — Anne Brontë

1.

Unless the rose
is thornless, the stem wine-
bottle smooth & burgundy—a scion singing
    pinot noir
    cabernet

Unless from that stem
the leaves fall like tendrils, laced & lancelot

      Unless the blooms are
     champagne
     double clustered—
heavy in their own delight

That is a rose worth craving
    & planting
      in an Arizona
mining camp   circa 1855

     The Chinese rose
dug deep by a Scottish bride is Tombstone

  (the outlaw town of the single
thornless tree in a desert
    otherwise drunk with thorns)

Rather: desert
     drunk
       with acacias
    that weave arroyos into wicked paths
    that cluster like outlaws

2.

Before the moon sleeps
with its lover
                                                Cereus
I want to memorize their names
            winter thorn
            sweet acacia
            river wattle
            guajillo
            cat claw
            tésota
            mimosa
            prickly Moses
            white thorn
            camel thorn
            desert carpet
            dead finish
                                        repeat

3.

Unless the rose is thornless
        my clippers
    would not sing
                the sheering
song—preserve the winter
                        sprig
captured from neighbor's yard—
        the full-moon night & leaves glossy
        if not glowing

Does this merlot branch reach
back to the bride's own bouquet?

                         Romantic
    the thought
                though untrue

Unless the thorn stems
from acacia
            & the spindle-tipped trellis
craves the Scottish cluster
of her heart wine-tinged & blooming
                &
                                    repeat

Opuntia

Abrajo: whose pads
           like daggers
shine & ignite
           a holy procession—
the roofless church
           of the desert
& the bleeding hills
           that swallow the red
eye of the sun.
           Some prefer: *vela
de coyote*, the candle—
           the white grin
of the moon—
           convinced (or else
drunk) it
           itself
is the sharpest tongue
           between the dark teeth
of the dawn.
           The night, un-
flattered, washes
           the world
to its bluest corners.
           Opuntia: prickly
pear, punctures
           the face of heaven,
where stars ascend
           like silver moths,
like the glowing
           souls of children.

Her Mission of Light

Seven months after the death of my mother,
the corpulent C-130s circling the air base

remind me how, when she was nine,
the Swedish girl they called *matchstick legs*

(who could sprint the sandy length
of seaside lane in record time) first heard

and then saw the Nazi bombers
in their razor-tight formations scraping

the low chin of the horizon, en route
to Norway and dark England beyond.

She too passed like a recondite
mission, whispering from 17,000 feet,

a near-anonymous entry into the endless log
of the world's migrations. Sixty-one years

later, I take the vacant road past
the base's back gate, along the brilliantly

destructive rows of F-4s and A-10s,
with their own secret missions to

Vietnam and Bosnia and Iraq, places
she could have lived in her 1950s

migration to America—places like the vast
and abundant plains of Rhodesia or

the golden avenues of Naples and Rome.
The street here is not glowing, nor

full of life. But it leads to the blue
hills beyond the river, and from there

the scarlet cliffs of the Santa Catalinas—
and sometimes, as now, the light off a curving

wing catches and holds the mountains and clouds
and, higher still, a vapor trail to the heavens.

3. Inflorescence

Inflorescence

1.

If her plunge through the plate window
was a blossom—glass shards
like petals peeled from the stem
of her body, slicing
air and flesh, breaking silence
upon silence—
then her fall was the quick scythe,
the awful noise
of realization as she crashed
from dark room to light,
wood floor to stone,
easy leap to hard, clear resistance.

I turned, thinking a cabinet had cracked,
a vase or saucer slipped. Instead
my daughter stood in the fractured aura
of a sliding glass door:
pale as a paper doll, eyes flat
and wide, blood inking the white
pages of her arms and legs.

She folded when I caught her.
The floor shimmered in ruby and silver:
my daughter's blood and the shrapnel
of the window.
My voice was not my own
but neither was hers.
I called for help as she chanted *O my god*—
her words warping my thoughts.

❧

The tourniquet: a mother's sheer blouse.
Bandages: kitchen towels.

Field medics: fathers and mothers
moving swiftly to raise her leg,
staunch the bleeding
and shield exposed bone:
finding the deep cuts: marking and splinting,
wrapping and soothing.
Her father was there and yet
I was not there, locked on those cerulean eyes,
singing *You're going to be fine, Sugarbug.*
You're doing so well, Sugarbug—knowing
I could not know.

That evening, my eleven-year-old
daughter past one surgery and waiting
for another, I returned
to the oval periphery of glass
a half-inch thick
that gaped like a mouth full
of bright teeth. A stained-glass image breathed
in and out. They could see her, too:
the mother and her daughters
who lived in the house and hosted the party.
Yet they never visited, never phoned or
wished her well: invisible
like a window closed but calling:
open, open.

2.

Our agave is dying:
a thick stalk rises on center
in bluegreen and mauve. Large
as a bull, the needle-edged plant wants
to bloom before toppling:
Who doesn't aspire to shine
before the end?
The fleshy branch

grows six inches wide
as it spires a foot a day.
In a week the candled tip meets roofline,
in two, claims twenty feet or more.

We view it from the park,
from the roundabout,
from the porch across the street. Only the desert
willow of the neighbor's yard is taller—
so sings a cardinal courting the day,
the dark owl gathering the night.

The inflorescence begins:
panicles shaped like tendons peel
from the stalk until resting, arms out:
fists become fingers,
fingers unfurl buds: a thousand
unopened flowers, moonlight green.
Then the wait—for the bats and hawkmoths
and for the full energy to flee its drying base,
risk roots' release
to satisfy the high thirst of that first
and final bloom that will sever
the heart of the agave
like glass cleaves light, pierces flesh:
the close, cold price of beauty.

3.

We did not know
my daughter's tendons had severed,
though the ghostly image
of naked bone floated before me,
though her blood filled the towels
and dyed the floor, her leg holding
even as ligaments coiled like wire
drawn tight then cut.

I remember a boy, a young man
really, trembling under the weight
of her leg, holding it high
before the ambulance arrived, the look
of fear in his dark eyes,
his arms stained and straining.
I remember my own trembling
as I feared to move, to shift her arm
or slide her punctured body,
to wipe the sweat from my chin
or blood from her cheek, to breathe too little
or too much.
I remember her breathing, shallow
and constant, like her talking.
And I remember the shock of my eyes
reflected in hers: the grace of the parents
beside us: the gleam of the chrome stretcher
once the paramedics arrived:
her slow rising, the many hands
under head and limbs:
the long ride to the hospital
and short call to my wife.

I remember hoping
my daughter would not recall
the nightmares following
the first operation,
when the surgeons drew out shards
like precious gems,
when they stitched her shin and knee knowing
tomorrow they'd reopen the wounds
to fish out the tendons and deeper glass.
She swam in and out of consciousness
in that endless emergency room hour,
pupils small as pencil leads:
Mommy daddy where are you?
    Right here, we said.

Why is the car moving?
    We're in the hospital.
Why is the room moving?
    It's not moving, honey.
Who is that, where are we, where are you?
Then the sobs before she'd sleep
a few minutes more:
Mommy daddy where are you?
    Right here, we said, right here—
anesthesia her bitter friend.

In the curtained cubicle next to us
a man moaned and flailed and then fell
quiet. Surgeons scrambled,
the bald doctor screamed for silence:
nurses slipped in and out
of the room as the biker who flew
in the last light of afternoon
before tumbling to the asphalt
moved no more.

My daughter woke
and did not recall her nightmares
though she would,
even among all that bright silence.

4.

Our agave is the pup
of the yard's first planting, cultivated
before its parent toppled from parasites
rather than blooms.
I cleaved thick leaves
to get to the core of the disease,
found nurseries of ravenous grubs
writhing in the sudden light,
the dark weevils scattering.

Burn them all
the natural history guide urged:
burn the grubs and insects, *cabeza* and leaves.
I had neither the heart nor the permit,
so set instead to exposing
the delicacies for thrasher and wren.
The quick birds sang
of their fortune, their black beaks stabbing
and stabbing the pungent delights.

Now I find the last offspring
of our dying agave and slice
beneath the blue rosette.
The white root severs sweetly,
like halving an apple
or pruning crisp stem.
You will replace your parent I say:
you will pierce the air like Agave of Thebes
pierces her only son, over and over, believing
the king is a beast: cruel trick
of the gods. They laugh as they fall
to the spiked desert floor.

5.

Is it right to say I slept
on the chair next to her hospital bed
when I could only recline, eyes pried,
and watch her body shift
in sporadic sleep? Was it wrong
to be wary of nightmares, mine as much as hers?
Would now be the time to pray
to indifferent gods?

By morning I believed
only in the precise schedule of nurses,
the persistence of fluorescent lights

and the doctor I met the day before.
Cool as a leading actor,
the orthopedic surgeon warned me
the operation could fail:
if tendons retreated beyond mending
or nerves negated, she might lose
the foot's function. He took
my hand, mentioned his daughter
of the same age and pointed me
to the lounge where visitors
gathered in twos and threes,
waiting out the diagnoses, huddled
in their own theaters of victory and defeat.

Not the leg wrapped and immobilized
nor the tubes draped like tendrils
from her body
nor even the black stitches
on head and shoulder, wrist and thigh.
Rather: her bruised eyes
and cracked lips warned me
before she woke.
I took her hand as her eyes found their focus:
no nightmares, but the pain:
Nine on a scale of ten she breathed
as the nurse increased her dosage
and the pain fled to her head
and she vomited
through the afternoon.

The surgery, though,
succeeded: the splint secured,
a walker and wheelchair reserved
so my daughter could begin moving
again through the hospital,
through the house,

through a summer now lost—
yet another season of childhood severed
by the swift blade of one hand
or another.

6.

The agave hoards carbohydrates
in its succulent heart,
gathering sugar and starch
as the leaves spike, each tip thin as a whip
scorpion, black as the widow
in her gauzy web.
For a decade our agave survived
searing summers and sudden
storms. Recall the December morning
the water pipes fused,
the remarkable January
snowfall, last August's clouds—
so bloated the agave's
swollen leaves must have punched
the torrents down.

If a heart, why not a brain
or the secretive soul?
Some species of the garden are that
familial: the saguaro in its top hat
of ivory blooms, an ocotillo slipping
into emerald gown after each brief storm—
and our agave with that buxom rosette: beguiling
but for those fingertip spikes:
not the aunt to rub elbows with
but the sharp-tongued sister
all mischief and delight.

Heavy in its own delight
or else weary

from the weight, the agave stalk leans
once inflorescence begins: retreating
from the roof, reaching
for the blue halls
above the street. With each new appendage
the limb sways further,
as if eager to walk after years
of attachment: a bloom-tipped cherub
or the virgin chalice, unopened.

7.

The scythe of her fall continued
to cull long after my daughter's return.
She endured wheelchair and walker
but faltered under the bruised plume
of darkness as her nightmares returned.
Each evening she tumbled into that foreign house,
adrift in the shadow line
between bright room and dark:
glass shattering then resealing, body folding
and unfolding.
Familiar faces likewise cleaved her:
eyes rimmed in white, they knew more
than they saw and saw more than they said.
She knew, too, how close the call—
a puncture this way or that, the wrist slit
a slight bit deeper…

Leg raised in a purple cast, my daughter
saddled her wheelchair
not as steed but as carriage,
her father the coachman and a reckless one at that:
galloping down the street, swerving
past puddles, cornering

like a barrel racer, wheels traded for hooves,
barrels imagined and real.
My plan to excise her dark
visions on track, she soon wheeled
herself along sidewalk and swale,
my legs scissoring beside her
as she leaned hard into the path.
Perhaps recovery is that way:
the flight to forget
fuels the fight to push forward
and forward again.

❦

After three weeks the surgeon cut away
my daughter's cast, exposing
her flesh and the black wound curving
across pale shin like a centipede—
each stitch a violet leg,
each segment a stain of dead skin
or angry scar. She turned away
despite the doctor's voice,
his guarantees that the cleft would fade
as he plucked the stitches
from ankle to knee and spun
the second cast in wild pink.

If we do not understand
that fairness dissolves
when healing comes to court
then we learn it fast: the task
of recovery tougher
than the injury itself. Was the pain
of that first step worse than her fear
of pain? Would her faith shatter
like untempered glass, shards
of doubt lodging in tissue and bone?
Or would she step through

unscathed, leg teetering
but still standing, hands locked
around the silver walker, head
and eyes raised in the afternoon light?

8.

The street teems with neighbors
the night the agave falls.
For days the winds heave
from the east, wrenching the monsoon
from the Santa Ritas, from the Huachucas,
from Mexico beyond.
They speak of scoured landscapes:
granite canyons, villages
of white adobe, mesquites ribboned
like broken diadems above underground streams.
Yet the winds promise rain
and the air is vibrant, expectant
as we step out of our homes
to accept the wind's flat hand,
to welcome its tattered sleeves.

There is little elegance
in the plant's collapse: already angled,
the heavy stalk and its chandelier
of buds level with a sick
thud, dry roots releasing, a shallow pocket
of earth where the agave once held:
a vacancy where the stalk rose.

The neighbor boy shouts
that the spire blocks the road, eager
for me to share in his delight
that traffic might back up for miles.
What a night! he says and I agree:
this is a night for reckoning

though the finale is not what I had planned,
though it seems I have always
planned for the season's swift scars.

From the garage I bring the saw
and measuring tape and return
to find children scaling the agave, climbing
over and under, weaving like night
geckos. Even my daughter takes
to the stalk, balancing
as if on a see-saw, her cast a bright marquee
against the shaft's dull veneer,
the walker beside her gleaming
in the moonlight. My younger daughter draws
the silver tongue of the tape
to the stalk's tip as I skirt
the sharp leaves and measure:
thirty-eight feet in all.

The tape retracts and the inflorescence
contracts and I expect my daughter likewise
to withdraw. Yet she calls me
to the stalk's first arm, still intact,
and asks me to cleave. She wants
I think some way to remember
the efflorescence cut short. But instead
she hopes the branch might recover:
already you can see the yellow-
tipped fingers, the nectared flowers
nearly open, and where
the inflorescence severs
Look there! she cries, pointing
at how it rises—
      how it blooms.

Notes

Shine
During summer Saturday evenings, the Arizona-Sonora Desert Museum west of Tucson, Arizona, stays open late so visitors may glimpse the desert—compressed into a sort of natural history museum meets zoo meets botanical gardens—at night. One of our favorite activities is "shining" scorpions with ultraviolet lights.

Bosque
The Bosque del Apache National Wildlife Refuge, nestled along the Rio Grande of central New Mexico, hosts one of the largest over-wintering populations of snow geese and Sand Hill cranes in North America.

Plastic
The Gyre is an area of the north Pacific Ocean near the Midway Atoll in which plastic has been collecting for years and is now twice the size of Texas. In autumn 2009, photographer Chris Jordan visited Midway to photograph the effects of plastic on albatrosses. View his beautifully horrific photographs at www.chrisjordan.com.

Amazon.com
Amazon.com, the online retailing giant, recommends items for you to purchase based on your history of items viewed, items you have previously purchased, and your movement through the website. Lukeville, Arizona, and Sonoyta (Sonora, Mexico) are adjoining border towns.

Flare
Arizona Highway 86 runs west from Tucson to Ajo, Arizona, just north of Organ Pipe Cactus National Monument and the Mexico border.

Home and Back Again
The Yaqui are a tribe of American Indians located in Sonora, Mexico, and southern Arizona. During Easter, Yaqui communities—in this case located a few miles south of downtown Tucson—hold celebrations that are a mix of their native religion and

Catholicism. The deer dance is the most sacred, and least integrated, of these rituals. The "flower world" is the sacred, parallel wilderness world of the Yaqui. Community members and outsiders alike may view the deer dance, which lasts all evening, but recording instruments such as cameras and pen and paper are not allowed.

Animal Logic
The three-line epigraph introducing this poem, a portion of an untitled Yaqui deer song, comes from *Yaqui Deer Songs ~ Maso Bwikam: A Native American Poetry*, by Larry Evers and Felipe S. Molina, an outstanding exploration of the Yaqui deer dancers and singers, published in 1987.

Box
Frank Gohlke is a preeminent modern landscape photographer and critic. I had the good fortune of taking a landscape photography theory and practice class under Frank in autumn 2008. The epigraph introducing this poem is from his 2007 book, *Accommodating Nature: The Photographs of Frank Gohlke*.

Dining in SoHo
SoHo is a neighborhood in Manhattan, New York City, known for its arts, shopping, and dining, sometimes referred to as "the biggest little village in the world." The poem is inspired by the form and approach of William Carlos Williams's poem "Franklin Square" (from *The Clouds*, 1948).

Sting
The Tumacacori valley, part of the Tumacacori Highlands, is located in Arizona northwest of the U.S.-Mexico border town of Nogales. Much of the Arizona-Sonora border—and much of the U.S.-Mexico border—is now severed by a high wall that may do little to keep "illegal immigrants" out of the U.S. but restricts the ability of wildlife to move across its natural range, including some species of native bees, which do not fly as high as the wall and so cannot cross it. The border region deserts of the U.S./Mexico and Israel/Palestine support more species of native bees than any other locations on Earth.

Thorn
Anne Brontë's epigraph introducing this poem is from her poem, "The Narrow Way." Tombstone is an "Old West" town in southeastern Arizona that is home to the original Tombstone rose, a thornless variety with white, yellow, or champagne-colored blooms cultivated by Mary Gee, the wife of mining engineer Henry Gee—newlyweds just arrived from Scotland. The "Lady Banks White Rose" variety, *Rosa banksiae banksiae*, not only survived, but thrived—the original rose is still alive today and, at more than 120 years old and 8,000 square feet, is considered the "world's largest rose."

Opuntia
Opuntia is the scientific genus name for the prickly pear cactus, of which there are roughly 200 species native to the Western hemisphere. *Abrajo* and *vela de coyote* are common Spanish names for certain Mexican species of prickly pear.

Her Mission of Light
The air base referenced in this poem is Davis-Monthan Air Force Base located in Tucson, Arizona. The base is home to what is commonly referred to as the Boneyard: the final resting place for decommissioned U.S. Air Force, Navy, and other helicopters and airplanes, including F-4 *Phantoms* predominantly used in the Vietnam conflict, and A-10 *Thunderbolts*, used in Bosnia, Iraq, and elsewhere.

Glossary

Agave
A succulent varying in size, usually with thick green, bluegreen, or graygreen leaves tipped in long, sharp spines. The leaves generate from a single rosette, though the plants may grow in clumps of two or three. The edges of the leaves may be serrated. Most agaves (pronounced *uh-gah-vay*) flower only once by sending up a rapidly growing bloomstalk; then they die. They reproduce by sending clones—called pups, offsets, or (in pre-Columbian legend) daughters—by underground shoots. They also may reproduce after the blooms appear en masse on the stalks (the inflorescence). Native to the desert regions of North and Central America and the Caribbean.

Arroyo
The traditional Spanish term for a shallow canyon or dry waterway or riverbed. In Arizona, generally referred to as a "wash." Contains water only during or after heavy rainfalls (pronounced *uh-roy-o*).

Bladderpod
A short pale to bright yellow flower that blooms in the spring rarely though profusely under the right conditions (i.e., a wet winter) throughout the Sonoran desert.

Bluestem
A wiry grass native to the American Great Plains and high desert regions of the American Southwest.

Brittlebush
A silvergreen shrub with deep yellow, daisylike flowers, native to the Sonoran desert.

Bosque
The traditional Spanish term for a heavily wooded area along wetlands and waterways, especially in arid regions such as the deserts of Arizona, New Mexico, and northern Mexico (pronounced *bo-skay*).

Cabeza
The Spanish term for "head," and also the term for the main portion—or body or heart—of the agave (pronounced *cuh-bay-zuh*).

Caliche
A dense, very hard subsoil clay common in southern Arizona (pronounced *cuh-leech-ay*).

Chicory
A graygreen plant with white, rough-edged daisylike flowers that blooms throughout the Sonoran desert in spring.

Chitinous
Referring to the hard and/or horny substance that makes up the exoskeleton of insects, arachnids, and arthropods.

Cichlid
A small, usually brightly-colored freshwater fish native to tropical regions of North and South America and Africa and common in the aquaria and pet store trades.

Cholla
A thin-branched and long-spiked cactus that may grow as large as a small tree, ranging in color from bright green to deep red (pronounced *choy-uh*).

Coral snake
A small, venomous snake found in tropical and desert regions of North America, distinctly colored in bands of red, yellow, and black.

Cottonwood
A large deciduous tree with green, glossy ovate leaves that turn bright yellow in autumn, found along waterways throughout the American West.

Creosote
A long-lived and airy shrub native to the Sonoran desert with small, waxy yellow-green leaves. The creosote releases a distinct aroma before rainstorms that is often referred to as "the smell of the desert."

Efflorescence
The state or period of flowering.

Gila flicker
More commonly referred to as the Gila (pronounced *hee-la*) woodpecker, an active woodpecker, native to the Sonoran desert, that often nests in saguaros.

Globemallow
A large, silvergreen perennial with small, saucer-shaped orange flowers, native to the Sonoran desert.

Indian paintbrush
A short plant with red, spiked flower clusters shaped somewhat like a grouping of paintbrushes, native to the western U.S.

Inflorescence
The arrangement of flowers on a single stem or stalk—specifically, in this case, the flowering stalk structure including branches (or panicles) and buds of an agave.

Lantana
A spreading, deep green-leafed plant with small clusters of brightly colored flowers (ranging from white to yellow, orange to purple) native to tropical regions of the world and introduced widely into the neighborhoods of Tucson, Arizona.

Mesquite
A wide, short, and woody tree with small, filtered leaves, native to the American Southwest, southern Great Plains, and dry regions of South America (pronounced *meh-skeet*).

Ocotillo
A tall, funnel-shaped plant native to the Sonoran and Chihuahuan deserts in which straight, spiked stems grow from a single base, leafless except after rain, with clusters of red flowers atop each stem. Not a cactus, the ocotillo (pronounced *o-ko-tee-o*) is often confused for one.

Palo verde
A wide and short, bright green-barked tree with small, filtered leaves that may drop in the hottest seasons, native to the Sonoran desert. The palo verde (pronounced *pal-o vair-day*) has small yellow flowers in spring.

Panicle
The stem or limb of an agave's bloomstalk, usually ending in many buds or blooms. A bloomstalk may contain no panicles, only a few, or several dozen, depending on the plant species.

Penstemon
A tall flowering perennial; the flowers are often red or pink, clustering along a spike, and are a favorite of hummingbirds.

Prickly pear
A generally low-growing cactus, usually green but sometimes purple, with wide, beaver-tail shaped pads and lots of spines. The fruit of the prickly pear ripens to a deep red or purple and is often harvested.

Ringtail
A catlike mammal the size of a housecat with a long banded tail, native to the Sonoran desert.

Roadrunner
A crested bird common in the American Southwest and about the size of a medium hawk, though thinner, with a long neck, sharp black beak, and long, rudderlike tail; so named because it prefers to run along the ground rather than fly.

Saguaro
A thick, single-trunked, pleated green cactus that may live up to 150 years or more and grow as high as 50 feet, often with multiple arms. The saguaro (pronounced *suh-whar-o*) grows in isolated scatterings and in large "forests" throughout the Sonoran desert. The cactus is known as the "sentinel of the desert."

Saxifrage
A small, matted flowering plant that can be found in moist, rocky locations.

Sonoran desert
The relatively lush desert region of the American Southwest ranging from southeast California through central Arizona and then south into Sonora and Baja California, Mexico. The Chihuahuan desert, which is less lush but contains more grasslands, borders the

Sonoran desert to the east, ranging from Arizona to New Mexico and western Texas, south into Mexico.

Wash
A shallow canyon or dry waterway or riverbed of the American Southwest; also called an arroyo. Contains water only during or after heavy rainfalls.

Yaqui
An American Indian tribe indigenous to Sonora, Mexico, and southern Arizona (pronounced *yah-kee*). See Notes for more information.

About the Author

SIMMONS B. BUNTIN is the American author of one previous book of poems, *Riverfall*, published by Salmon Poetry in 2005. His award-winning poetry and prose have appeared in numerous North American and European journals and anthologies. He is the founding editor of the acclaimed international journal *Terrain.org: A Journal of the Built & Natural Environments*, for which he also writes a regular editorial. He is the recipient of the Colorado Artists Fellowship for Poetry, an Academy of American Poets prize, and grants by the Arizona Commission on the Arts and Tucson Pima Arts Council. He is an avid photographer, website designer, and all-around rabble-rouser who lives with his wife and two daughters in the Sonoran desert of southern Arizona. Catch up with him at www.simmonsbuntin.com.

Digital Resources

In addition to the resources available on the Salmon Poetry website at www.salmonpoetry.com, access audio and video readings and links to information contained within many of the poems in *Bloom* at www.simmonsbuntin.com/bloom.